Pebble® Plus

Animal Groups

A Colony of Bees

by Lucia Raatma

PEBBLE
a capstone imprint

Pebble Plus is published by Pebble, a Capstone imprint, 1710 Roe Crest Drive, North Mankato, Minnesota 56003 www.mycapstone.com

Library of Congress Cataloging-in-Publication Data
Names: Raatma, Lucia, author.
Title: A colony of bees / by Lucia Raatma.
Description: North Mankato, Minnesota : Pebble, [2020] | Series: Animal groups | Includes bibliographical references and index. | Audience: Age 5-7. | Audience: K to Grade 3.
Identifiers: LCCN 2019003017| ISBN 9781977109477 (library binding) | ISBN 9781977110435 (paperback) | ISBN 9781977109538 (ebook pdf)
Subjects: LCSH: Bees—Behavior—Juvenile literature. | Social behavior in animals—Juvenile literature.
Classification: LCC QL569.4 .R33 2020 | DDC 595.79/9—dc23
LC record available at https://lccn.loc.gov/2019003017

Editorial Credits
Abby Colich, editor; Tracy McCabe, designer; Eric Gohl, media researcher; Kathy McColley, production specialist

Photo Credits
Alamy: Scott Camazine, 15; Shutterstock: Azami Adiputera, 17, Banthoon Saeko, 11, bluedog studio, 19, Daniel Prudek, cover (isolated bee), Dredger, 13, Feri Istanto, back cover (bottom), 5, Ihor Bondarenko, 21, Pedro Turrini Neto, 7, rtbilder, cover, 1, StockMediaSeller, back cover (top), 9, StudioSmart, 2, background

All internet sites appearing in back matter were available and accurate when this book was sent to press.

Note to Parents and Teachers

The Animal Groups set supports national science standards related to life science. This book describes and illustrates life in a colony of bees. The images support early readers in understanding the text. The repetition of words and phrases helps early readers learn new words. This book also introduces early readers to subject-specific vocabulary words, which are defined in the Glossary section. Early readers may need assistance to read some words and to use the Table of Contents, Glossary, Read More, Internet Sites, Critical Thinking Questions, and Index sections of the book.

Printed in the United States   6073

Table of Contents

What Is a Colony?

Buzz! A bee zooms by.

It is taking food to its colony.

A colony is a group of bees

that live together.

A colony lives in a nest.
Bees build these homes.
Nests are in trees or in
the ground. Some are under
roofs or other covered areas.

Bee Jobs

Each bee has a job. Most colonies
have one queen. Her job is
to lay eggs. Drones are males.
They mate with the queen.
The queen lays many eggs.

queen bee

Worker bees are female.
They do many jobs. Some search
for food. They gather pollen
and nectar from flowers.
They take it back to the nest.

Workers also feed and
take care of young bees.
They feed and clean the queen.
Some workers clean the nest.
Others guard it.

young

worker bee

Working Together

Some bees dance to tell others where to find food. They dance in the shape of an 8. The longer they dance, the farther away the food is.

Guard bees protect the entrance of the nest. They watch out for predators. Some bees sting predators. Other bees bite them.

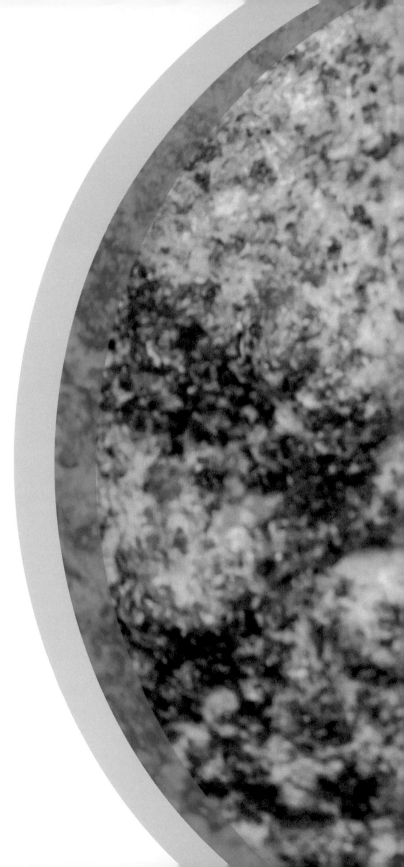

Some colonies get too crowded. The queen and some workers leave the nest. They build a new home. The old nest gets a new queen.

The Need for Bees

People need bees. Bees spread pollen from plant to plant. This helps plants grow. People use those plants for food. They also use the honey that some bees make.

Glossary

mate—to join together to produce young

nectar—a sweet liquid found in many flowers

nest—a home where animals live and raise young

pollen—a powder made by flowers to help them create new seeds

predator—an animal that hunts another animal for food

Read More

Esbaum, Jill. *Honey Bees*. Explore My World. Washington, D.C.: National Geographic Kids, 2017.

Marsh, Laura. *Bees*. Washington, D.C.: National Geographic, 2016.

Unstead, Sue. *Amazing Bees*. New York: DK Publishing, 2016.

Internet Sites

Easy Science for Kids
https://easyscienceforkids.com/learn-about-bees-video-for-kids/

Pest World for Kids
https://pestworldforkids.org/pest-guide/bees/

San Diego Zoo Kids: Bees
https://kids.sandiegozoo.org/animals/bee

Super-cool stuff! Check out projects, games, and lots more at **www.capstonekids.com**

Critical Thinking Questions

1. What are some of the jobs of worker bees?
2. What happens when a nest gets too crowded?
3. Why do people need bees?

Index